Voices of CONSEQUENCES
ENRICHMENT SERIES

Unlocking the Prison Doors

(12 Points to Inner Healing and Restoration)

BY: JAMILA T. DAVIS
VOLUME 1

Workbook/Journal

VOICES
INTERNATIONAL PUBLICATIONS

Voices of Consequences Enrichment Series
Unlocking the Prison Doors: 12 Points to Inner Healing and Restoration Workbook/Journal

This book is a nondenominational, faith-based, instruction manual. It was created to inspire, uplift and encourage incarcerated women to overcome the dilemmas that led to their imprisonment and to provide instructions to help them obtain emotional healing. The author shares the strategies she has utilized, both spiritual and non-spiritual, to gain emotional wholeness. This book is not written to promote any set of religious beliefs, although it does encourage readers to be open to receiving assistance from their "Higher Power" as they know Him.

The author of this book does not claim to have originated any techniques or principles shared in this book. She has simply formulated a system of proven strategies, from her research and experience during imprisonment, that her readers can utilize to obtain healing and restoration. A comprehensive list of references used to create this work is located in the back of this book. Readers are encouraged to use this reference list to obtain additional books to further their learning experience.

Printed in the United States of America
First Printing, 2012

Library of Congress Control Number: 2012941665
ISBN: 978-0-9855807-1-1

Voices International Publications
196-03 Linden Blvd.
St. Albans, NY 11412
"Changing Lives A Page At A Time."
www.vocseries.com

Typesetting and Design by: Jana Rade www.impactstudiosonline.com
Edited by: Ann Lockwood, Kat Masurak and Theresa Squillacote

INTRODUCTION

The *Voices of Consequences Enrichment Series* was created to help incarcerated women successfully rehabilitate and heal from past wounds. It is the goal of this series to assist women to succeed, enabling them to transition back into society and overcome the stigma of being an ex-convict.

The first book in this series, entitled *Unlocking the Prison Doors* focuses on self-discovery, understanding character flaws and weaknesses, identifying the roots of those difficulties, and developing avenues of solutions. It is an intense journey that takes women through the process of shedding guilt, shame, regret, and low self-esteem. It challenges women to accept the past, to learn from it, and to let it go. These lessons are invaluable and essential in helping incarcerated women rehabilitate.

The Workbook/Journal illuminates the content of the textbook through practice, so that women actively pursue their own growth. Examples are provided to help women recognize their similar tendencies and weaknesses—the first step in the change process. The textbook, along with the Workbook/Journal, is a powerful tool with the ability to create significant change within the user.

This series is unique in nature. This self-help expert, author Jamila T. Davis, is an inmate writing in a voice of care and compassion that other inmates can relate to. Davis provides the road map she used to overcome the dilemmas that she faced during imprisonment. She skillfully directs her readers to see their crimes from the viewpoint of their victims, helping them genuinely to accept responsibility for their actions, and yet at the same time to open their hearts for healing and restoration.

Using This Workbook/Journal

In your hand, you hold the Workbook/Journal for *Unlocking the Prison Doors*, Volume One of the *Voices of Consequences Enrichment Series*. This Workbook was designed to help you, through practice, deepen your understanding of the content in *Unlocking the Prison Doors*. Use this Workbook to record and track your healing process. As you begin to chronicle your experiences, you will discover not only areas in your life that require change, but also areas where you are making significant improvements.

Participation through use of the Workbook/Journal helps you process the information you have read in the textbook. It is an essential part of the healing process. As you record your experiences and re-read them, they will direct you to the root of many long-term difficulties that may have been blocking and delaying your success.

Growth and self-discovery can be a slow process. Take your time going through the exercises in this Workbook/Journal. Read the appropriate chapter in the *Unlocking Prison Doors* textbook first. Study the information you read in the text, then answer the questions in this Workbook/Journal and complete the exercises.

In the back of this Workbook/Journal is a Journal section where you can write about your progress and take notes on the discoveries you have made while reading the text. The greater detail you can add to your journaling the easier it will be to identify areas needing change. The Journal will also help you to track your progress as you re-read what you have written.

Healing and restoration do not happen overnight. The process requires work! The level of personal effort you employ will determine your progress. Take the necessary time to read the text and make the most honest evaluation of "self." Be consistent with this project. Use these books throughout your journey of change. You will be amazed when seeing how much progress you can make by being diligent with your studies.

If you are struggling to answer the questions in this Workbook/Journal, refer back to the text. Review the chapter in the text until you are able to fully comprehend the information. Then, return to this Workbook/Journal. Take this experience seriously, and answer the questions as accurately and truthfully as you can. As you do so, you will gain tremendous insight into "self."

Keep this Workbook/Journal in a safe place. Occasionally review your previous answers and writings. This exercise will allow you to gauge how far you have advanced, and the process will keep you focused on what is needed to remain on the right path. Enjoy the journey.

CHAPTER 1 REVIEW
Learning to Surrender

The first step we must take in our journey to healing and restoration is to surrender. To surrender is to give up attachment to results as we expect them. In order to successfully embark upon this journey, we must release our attachment to how we believe things should happen in the external world and be more concerned with what happens inside of us.

To surrender is to accept that our lives have become unmanageable in the current state. Surrendering is to accept the way we have been living has not produced the results we desired. To surrender is the ability to put away our self-absorbed plans and to be open to new patterns of living that will make life more manageable.

To complete this journey, we must possess the willingness to change. Willingness is the ability to be open to new directions and a new lifestyle. Willingness cannot occur until we decide to surrender.

This chapter lays the groundwork for us to open our minds and to accept a new way of thinking. It opens the doors for us to realistically assess the way we have been living and to determine if we have the will to change.

Chapter Questions

1) What does it mean to surrender?

_____

_____

_____

_____

2) Why is it necessary to surrender in order to move forward in life?

_____

_____

_____

_____

3) Why does it take people a long time to surrender?

_____

_____

_____

_____

4) Why is it difficult to give up control?

_____

_____

_____

_____

5) How do you surrender?

_____

_____

_____

_____

6) What experiences or hardships have you endured that are similar to those expressed in the poem, "I Surrender- A Prisoner's Cry?"

_____

_____

_____

7) What mistakes did you make that led to your imprisonment?

_____

_____

_____

_____

8) What warnings did you have that should have alerted you to the need to change but which you ignored?

_____

_____

_____

_____

9) If you stay on the same track as you were before you were incarcerated, how do you think your life will turn out?

_____

_____

_____

_____

10) Do you have a need to surrender your old way of life? If so, write out some of the activities or actions you were involved with that you will need to give up. Then write why you need to give them up.

_____

_____

_____

_____

_____

_____

_____

_____

_____

_____

_____

_____

_____

Example

Regina was sentenced to 37 months in a federal prison for identity theft. For 5 years prior to her imprisonment, Regina lived off of information profiles of doctors that she illegally obtained. Regina lived a life of pleasure and luxury, using the identities of distinguished doctors. She bought a new car and a condo in Atlanta, GA, her hometown. Everything was great until the Feds uncovered her scam.

Regina was indicted and all of her property was confiscated, because it was gained by illegal means. Regina's new home is the Federal Correctional Institution in Danbury, CT. Imprisoned, Regina was forced to examine her choices and her way of life. Regina's options were simple: Stay the same, or make a change.

Regina contemplated going back on the streets and engaging in the same illegal activities in a bigger way to make up for her "losses" incurred during her incarceration. She thought about settling down and returning to school. She also thought about finding a way to legitimately support the lifestyle she desired.

Regina wanted to do the right thing, but she feared going back into the world, to struggle and to face the negative views others may have of her. Regina was accustomed to being on top, and she dreaded going back into society as an underdog.

As she continued to examine her choices, and considered the negative consequences of imprisonment, Regina worked up the courage to change her old way of life and her old way of thinking. She decided she did not want to make prison a part of her future. Regina opted to surrender. She is now a part of the *Voices of Consequences* program.

1) What kind of lifestyle did Regina live before she was incarcerated?

_____

_____

_____

_____

2) What choices did Regina contemplate while imprisoned?

_____

_____

_____

_____

3) What choice did Regina finally decide to make? Why?

_____

_____

_____

_____

4) With Regina's choice, what is left for her to do?

_____

_____

_____

_____

5) How is your situation or your choices similar or different to Regina's?

_____

_____

_____

_____

Writing Assignment - Journal Entry #1

Explain some of the activities you were involved in which you will need to surrender and why you need to surrender them.

_____

_____

_____

_____

_____

_____

_____

_____

_____

_____

_____

_____

_____

_____

_____

_____

_____

_____

_____

_____

_____

_____

_____

_____

_____

_____

_____

_____

_____

_____

_____

_____

_____

_____

CHAPTER 2 REVIEW
Accepting Help from Our "Higher Power"

Each of us has access to divine help from our "Higher Power" that lies within. He is the Being that sculpted, molded, and created us. To many of us, our "Higher Power" is known as the Almighty God. We can count on our "Higher Power" for strength, direction, and help, especially in our time of need.

Hardships exist so that we can be led to discover our relationship with our "Higher Power." During difficult times, we may come to realize that, as humans, we have no control over our lives, and we can do nothing without God. When we arrive at that realization, we are able to surrender our will and discover the will of God.

Obstacles teach us what is, and what is not, important in life. Preoccupied with the external world, many of us have had our priorities out of order. We have put our trust in people, places, and things, and this external focus has taken precedence in our lives. Not until we hit rock bottom do we realize how out of line our priorities have been! Our focus should never be on people, places, or things. Hardships teach us that our focus and trust need to be in our "Higher Power."

We are not alone in this journey! Our "Higher Power" within desires to help us. God has been talking to us through events, people, dreams, and thoughts. However, we were so busy in the world that we could not hear what He was saying. Now we must take the time to slow down and listen to the directions that God is giving us during this season of our lives.

God is a Gentleman, He doesn't force His way into our lives. He quietly waits for us to open the door for His help. When we surrender our will, we invite God into our lives to help us.

Many of us have been stuck, stagnated, because we have not invited God's intervention into our lives. God is all knowing! He holds all the solutions to life in His hands. The key to restoration is the willingness to surrender and open our minds and hearts to request help from our "Higher Power."

Chapter Questions

1) Who is our "Higher Power?"

_____

_____

_____

_____

2) Why do we need a "Higher Power" to get through this journey?

_____

_____

_____

_____

3) Why do people get angry at God?

_____

_____

_____

_____

4) How can we receive help from God? What does He require of us?

_____

_____

_____

_____

5) How can our time in prison become an opportunity?

_____

_____

_____

_____

6) Do we need the assistance of anyone other than ourselves to connect with our "Higher Power"? Why or why not?

_____

_____

_____

_____

7) What is God's purpose for obstacles?

_____

_____

_____

_____

8) How does God communicate with us? In what ways?

_____

_____

_____

_____

9) When does God give us the blessings He promises? What does He require first?

_____

_____

_____

_____

10) Why is it dangerous to put our hope and faith in people, places or things?

_____

_____

_____

_____

Example

Jennifer grew up in Milwaukee, Wisconsin in a good home. She learned about God from her parents, and she developed a positive relationship with Him as a child.

Jennifer was a good girl growing up. She tried her best to do the right thing at all times. All was well with Jennifer until she fell in love with Rakim. Rakim ran a major drug operation in Racine, Wisconsin. Jennifer's love for Rakim caused her to follow his ways. Jennifer, as the drug dealer's main girlfriend, joined Rakim's operation and began to enjoy the fruits of the money they made together.

Jennifer quickly became caught up in her new lifestyle. She broke away from her family and moved to Racine with Rakim. All was well until an informant set up Jennifer and Rakim. As a result, Jennifer was arrested and locked up in the county jail, and faced a 20-year sentence.

Jennifer was so distressed. She was only 20 years old and could be given a sentence that was as long as she had been on the Earth. Hopeless, Jennifer called her parents, who came to see her on visiting day. Tears streamed down Jennifer's face at the sight of her mother, whom she hadn't seen in over 3 years. Jennifer's mother suggested that Jennifer pray.

Jennifer decided to take her mother's advice, and she began to pray. At first, she felt like a hypocrite because she had abandoned her relationship with God since she left home. She cried out to Him, explaining her faults and failings. As Jennifer began to pray, she felt stronger and more able to face her challenges.

Jennifer reunited with her mom, and Jennifer's mother began to see her on a regular basis. During one of the visits, Jennifer's mother told Jennifer to become more specific with God and to ask Him directly for what she needed.

Jennifer took her mother's advice and began to pray specifically for what she desired. Jennifer had amazing results almost immediately! She learned to pray for even the small things she desired, and they began to show up in her life.

Jennifer stayed at the county jail for 10 months, and then she was sentenced to sixty months, slightly less than 4 years with good time credit.

Jennifer was happy about her reduced sentence, but she still had no clue how she would manage in prison.

During her time in prison, Jennifer maintained her relationship with God, Who guided her every step of the way. It was in her hours of greatest distress that Jennifer learned how to trust God.

Jennifer is now out of prison. She recently married and is expecting her first child. Today, Jennifer and her mother are best friends. Jennifer and her husband own a successful construction company. She is now making a comfortable living — legally! Jennifer is happy and at peace. Today she vows to never neglect her greatest relationship, with her "Higher Power." He has proven to be faithful to her!

1) Where did Jennifer go wrong? Why?

_____

_____

_____

_____

2) Why did Jennifer feel reluctant about turning back to God?

_____

_____

_____

_____

3) How did Jennifer communicate with her "Higher Power?"

_____

_____

_____

_____

4) What happened as a result of Jennifer's prayers?

_____

_____

_____

_____

5) Why is it important to be specific when you pray?

_____

_____

_____

_____

Writing Assignment- Journal Entry #2

Write a letter to your "Higher Power." Tell Him how you feel and what you expect or want Him to do in your life. Be specific.

_____

_____

_____

_____

_____

_____

_____

_____

_____

_____

_____

_____

_____

_____

_____

_____

_____

_____

_____

_____

_____

_____

_____

_____

_____

_____

_____

_____

_____

_____

CHAPTER 3 REVIEW

Getting to the Root of the Problem – "Who Am I?"

We live in a society where many people aren't happy with who they are. Buying into the standards of society, they are consumed by chasing a false basis for self-worth, comparing themselves with others who they believe are happy and successful. As a result, many people move through life behind masks. Insecure in their identities, they hide behind the mask of another persona.

Prison life magnifies this lost identity syndrome. It is common to see inmates hiding behind a false persona, believing that their mask will bring attention and recognition from others. Desperate for love and acceptance, many inmates are willing to live a lie to receive affirmation and praise from others.

Restoration cannot occur until we remove our masks. When we unwrap the layers of false identities that encumber us, we can finally ascertain who we truly are. Removing our mask can be a very painful process. Exposing our true "self" uncovers the wounds we so desperately tried to hide to relieve us of our pain. Removing our mask also means we reveal our insecurities. This process may initially cause us to feel naked and helpless, because we are forced to face reality. Our reality, in many cases, is frightening, so we avoid dealing with the truth of our dilemmas.

In order to heal, to become whole, and to live life to our fullest potential, we must be willing to remove our masks. We cannot move forward until we truthfully analyze "self" and get to the root of who we truly are.

Each of us was put on this Earth for a purpose. God bestows us with unique gifts and talents to fulfill our purpose here on Earth. We will not discover true fulfillment until we find our purpose. Life is a series of tests and obstacles that lead us to that ultimate purpose.

Each of us has a common spiritual enemy. He is the enemy of our souls. His assignment is to steal, kill, and destroy, to distract us and keep us from fulfilling our purpose. The enemy is patient and deceptive in his plans. He plots and schemes against us from the day we are born. He strategically designs mishaps to impair and disable us from becoming the people God intended us to be. Many of us were hurt as children, an intentional plan of the enemy. He planned our inflicted pain to throw us off the right course of life. His mission was to distract our minds and to distort our thinking, ultimately causing our destruction. Now that we know the plots and plans of the enemy, we must avoid his traps at all cost. We do that by opening our hearts and minds, so we have the ability to tear down the negative strongholds in our minds. These negative strongholds are called "stinking thinking."

In order to move forward, we must take a step back. We must examine how we became the person we are today. We must take a trip back in time and deal with the negativity that was sent to defile us. As we eliminate that negativity, we destroy the traps that have kept us bound.

Many of us have been abused as children. Abuse includes physical and mental damage inflicted on us by others. Children come into the world innocent and open-minded. The experiences a child endures molds her into who she will become. Children can easily pick up wrong thinking patterns. Just as they learn to speak by listening to adults around them, they learn negative behavioral patterns by watching those adults. Children adapt to the lifestyles and habits of those around them. Without proper love, care, and attention, children can follow the wrong path in life. Some of us have suffered abuse or neglect as a child and we do not realize the effects it has had on us. As a result, many of us have built walls of protection to avoid experiencing more pain. We have become products of our environments, blind to the root of our dilemmas. Some of us have blamed ourselves for what we have endured as children. No child is responsible for the abuse she suffers, but that isn't an excuse to remain stagnant in life. We must analyze the roots of our problems and then uproot them. When we break the strongholds that ensnare us, we become free. This is an important part of the process of healing and restoration.

One of our greatest delusions in life is that our happiness comes from people, places, and things. Experiencing the pains *OF* life, we subconsciously conclude that fulfillment must come from an experience *IN* life. Seeking fulfillment from that which is external, we depend on others or things for what only God can do. We become empowered when we align our thinking with that of our "Higher Power" and get to know our "self."

Many of us have been so involved in making others happy that we have lost touch with "self." We adopted others' dreams and sources of happiness as our own, neglecting what truly makes us happy. In this journey, it is important that we learn the truth of who we are, free from the views and concepts of others.

A common issue among female inmates is codependency. We believe we are alone or incomplete without having a person beside us every step of the way. When we have a false basis of self-worth and are guided by the world's views and values, we are not complete inside. We use people, places, and things to compensate for the emptiness inside. We become dependent on others and their emotions, and this dependency gives us a false sense of self-worth. Our lives become consumed with living up to the standards of the people upon whom we have grown dependent. We will do anything we can to gain their praise and attention.

Codependent behavior is self-destructive. Rather than being led by God, we are led by people. Many of our crimes and misjudgments were done in order to please someone else.

The only solution to codependency is detachment. For some of us, prison is the "time out" we need to rearrange our priorities and work on "self." We must not fear being alone! We now know we have the help of our "Higher Power." He is our Source of strength and provision. As we align ourselves with God, we no longer have the need to put our trust and hope in people. Instead, we place our trust in God, and He will lead us to the true fulfillment that arrives when we discover our purpose.

Throughout this journey, we will reveal the root of our dilemmas, which began with neglect of "self." As we discard our "stinking thinking," we discover the truth of who we are. Our goal is to rid ourselves of the self-made masks that we have used to cover our wounds, and to step into wholeness of mind, body, and soul.

Chapter Questions

1) Why are many of us not happy with ourselves?

_____

_____

_____

_____

2) Why is it easy to get caught up in a false identity of "self?"

_____

_____

_____

_____

3) How do childhood experiences affect who we are today?

_____

_____

_____

_____

4) Why are children easily influenced?

_____

_____

_____

_____

5) What is codependency?

_____

_____

_____

_____

6) Why does prison life often cause people to pretend to be someone other than who they are?

_____

_____

_____

_____

7) Why must we take off our mask and come out of denial in order to heal?

_____

_____

_____

_____

8) What is the job of the enemy of our souls? How does he work?

_____

_____

_____

_____

9) How do we achieve true fulfillment in life?

_____

_____

_____

_____

10) Why is it self-destructive to place our hope and faith in people, places and things?

_____

_____

_____

_____

Example

Elizabeth grew up in a rural area outside of St. Louis, Missouri. Elizabeth's parents died in a car accident when she was 4 years old, so she lived with her aunt and uncle.

By the time Elizabeth was seven years old, she was sexually abused by her uncle. Her aunt suspected something was wrong, but instead of helping Elizabeth, she blamed Elizabeth for her husband's destructive actions. Elizabeth's aunt began to verbally abuse her as well.

Elizabeth grew up in misery, tormented by abuse. She felt shameful and guilty about all that had occurred. As a result, Elizabeth suffered from a lack of self-esteem.

At the age of 16, Elizabeth met a man, George, who promised her a better life. Elizabeth, hoping to escape her past, chose to leave town with George, and together they moved to Kansas City, Missouri.

George quickly targeted Elizabeth's weaknesses and insecurities, and he used them to control her. George became very abusive to Elizabeth, crushing the last bit of self-esteem she possessed. George was an alcoholic, and he beat Elizabeth when he got drunk. One day he beat her so viciously that she collected all of her belongings and left him.

Elizabeth was homeless, with no family support. While living in the streets, she met a man, James, who introduced her to prostitution. James became Elizabeth's pimp, and she made a lot of money in the streets as a call-girl.

Prostitution became Elizabeth's way of life. She finally felt she had power and control over her destiny! For the first time in her life she made her own money, and she was proud of her ability to support herself.

One day, while turning a trick, her customer tried to rob her. He hit Elizabeth with heavy blows to the head. Her life threatened, Elizabeth began to fight back. She had so much anger and rage built up inside from years of abuse that she struck and killed the man with her bare hands.

Elizabeth was charged with manslaughter and sentenced to 10 years in prison. Despair overcame her, and Elizabeth believed that her life was over. She felt hopeless and worthless after all she had endured in life.

Upon entering prison, she was required to participate in the *Voices of Consequences* program to help her in the healing process. Elizabeth was shocked to discover that her life and her misfortunes were not all her fault. She was able to see how her abuse as a child played a large part in who and what she became. As she made these discoveries, she began to identify her "stinking thinking." She was able to get to the root of her problem as she worked on improving "self."

Today Elizabeth is whole! She has tremendously increased her self-esteem, and she finally believes in herself. She is currently enrolled in a

UNLOCKING THE PRISON DOORS

Culinary Arts program in prison and is also obtaining her college degree in Business Administration. She is determined to overcome the obstacles of her past and live a new abundant life. She is finally on the road to achieving her purpose.

1) What kind of abuse did Elizabeth endure as a child?

_____

_____

_____

_____

2) Was the abuse Elizabeth received as a child her fault? Why or why not?

_____

_____

_____

_____

3) Why was Elizabeth so willing to escape with George? Was she at fault for her decision?

_____

_____

_____

_____

4) How did Elizabeth get caught up in prostitution?

_____

_____

_____

_____

5) Were Elizabeth's misfortunes all her fault? Why or why not?

_____

_____

_____

_____

Writing Assignment- Journal Entry #3

Write an assessment of your childhood. List significant events in your life; describe how they made you feel at the time, and how they ultimately affected your life. Provide details.

_____

_____

_____

_____

_____

_____

_____

_____

_____

_____

_____

_____

_____

_____

_____

_____

_____

_____

_____

_____

_____

_____

_____

_____

_____

_____

_____

Chapter 4 Review
Acknowledging Our Shortcomings

In order for us to heal and advance in life, we must acknowledge our shortcomings. No one wants to admit her inadequacies. As humans, we like to believe we are operating smoothly. Acknowledging our shortcomings can be challenging and painful, causing many to avoid at all cost being truthful with themselves!

Denial is deadly because it offers no room to change. We cannot change until we are willing to admit that we have a problem. Many of us choose to stay in denial because we are afraid of what others may think about us. Instead of dusting off our defilements and fixing "self," we bury the truth of who we are by putting on the masks of denial.

We cannot fully heal until we are willing to expose the truth. The truth is exposed when we acknowledge the mistakes we made in the past and position ourselves to make the necessary adjustments to overcome them. It becomes easy to acknowledge our faults when we recognize the truth that our past mistakes are not failures; they are, in fact, just practiced success. We all have to learn and there is no better teacher than experience! Our experiences provide the road map we need to make the necessary corrections to achieve success.

In order to accurately pinpoint our shortcomings, we must journey back into our past. As we honestly evaluate our past behaviors, we can accurately diagnose what needs to be changed.

Journeying back in time requires us to look at our upbringing and highlight negative influences on our lives. In order to heal, we must identify just where we went wrong. As we look at past events, we are enlightened to the truth of our adverse behavioral patterns.

Many of us have blamed others for our past poor judgments rather than ourselves. We created many excuses to avoid dealing with the root of our problems. It is only when we are willing to be mature, to face the reality of our circumstances, and to accept responsibility for our wrongdoings that change will finally come! Accepting responsibility brings about a release. It unlocks us from the trap of denial and allows us to correct our vision, so that we can successfully move forward.

When we accept responsibility for our actions and examine our past behavioral patterns and, weaknesses, we are able to take a fearless moral inventory of ourselves. A moral inventory helps us to pinpoint areas of weaknesses as well as areas of strength.

As well as assessing our weaknesses, we must also analyze and recognize the negative influences we have had in our lives. Negative people contaminate us with their "stinking thinking." Subconsciously or consciously, we pick up their beliefs and ways of thinking, which we eventually take on as our own.

Negative people pull us down and take us off our correct course in life. They distract us from our goals and cause our progress to stagnate. Life may be fine until we are sucked in by the negative influences of another. Our desire to please or appease others can lead us astray and put us on a path that we don't wish to follow.

It is vital that we constantly check our surroundings and evaluate the motives of those around us. If people do not encourage us to be our best or promote our newfound purpose in life, they are negative influences, and we must rid ourselves of them. We become better people when we are surrounded by positivity. Positive people alert us when we are heading off course and lead us back to the correct road in life. They become walls of protection, helping to keep us from harm and danger.

When we accurately recognize negative people, we need to excise them from our lives in a loving manner. As we do so, the change in our atmosphere becomes quickly apparent.

Letting go of people we love can be a challenging task. Oftentimes we believe we can't live without certain people. This is not true. We can't let any person control or endanger our lives. We master whatever we are able to walk away from. Detaching simply means we give ourselves and that person space and time to grow. It doesn't mean we don't love them; it just means we are now taking care of ourselves by ourselves . As we learn how to rid ourselves of character flaws and codependency, we become free!

Instructions: Read the questions below carefully and then check the answer that best describes your actions

Moral Inventory List of Weaknesses

SECTION #1

1) Do you blame yourself for negative events that have happened in your past?
Yes ☐   No ☐

2) Do you feel ashamed of the events that have occurred in your life?
Yes ☐   No ☐

3) Do you often wish you could go back in your past and rewind time to fix the areas where you went wrong?
Yes ☐   No ☐

4) Do you ever wish you were never born because of the way your life has turned out?
Yes ☐   No ☐

If you answered "yes" to one or more of the questions in this section, you may be dealing with issues of shame and guilt.

SECTION #2

5) When you look in the mirror, do you like what you see?
Yes ☐   No ☐

6) Do you feel confident about yourself and the direction in which you are going in life?
Yes ☐   No ☐

7) Do you constantly compare yourself with others around you and measure your standards against theirs?
Yes ☐   No ☐

8) Do you wish you could be someone else?
Yes ☐   No ☐

If you answered "yes" to one or more of these questions in this section, you may be dealing with issues of self-pity and low self-esteem.

SECTION #3:

9) Do you blame a particular person or group of people for how your life turned out?
Yes ☐   No ☐

10) Do you often replay in your mind the pain that another has inflicted upon you?
Yes ☐   No ☐

11) Are you angry with someone who has hurt you in the past?
Yes ☐   No ☐

12) Do you have rage and anger that appears quickly when someone does something to you?
Yes ☐   No ☐

If you answered "yes" to one or more of the questions in this section, you may be dealing with issues of anger, resentment and unforgiveness.

SECTION #4:

13) Do you feel sad or lonely?
Yes ☐   No ☐

14) Do you cry when you think about your life and all that has happened to you?
Yes ☐   No ☐

15) Is it hard for you to be motivated to move forward in life because you feel heavily burdened by the weight of your problems?
Yes ☐   No ☐

16) Are you confused about what your next phase of life will be?
Yes ☐   No ☐

If you answered "yes" to one or more of the questions in this section, you may be dealing with issues of depression and frustration.

SECTION #5

17) Do you highly value what others say or think about you?
Yes ☐   No ☐

18) Do you often seek the advice of another person before you make a decision?
Yes ☐   No ☐

19) Do you often try your best to keep those whom you love or others around you happy?
Yes ☐   No ☐

20) Are you uncomfortable when you are not in a relationship with a significant other?
Yes ☐   No ☐

If you answered "yes" to one or more questions in this section, you may be dealing with issues of codependency and insecurity.

SECTION #6:

21) Are you afraid of what the future holds for you?
   Yes ☐   No ☐

22) Are you frightened to take on new challenges?
   Yes ☐   No ☐

23) Do you worry about what may or may not happen in the future?
   Yes ☐   No ☐

24) Are you afraid of what others may think if you fail at a challenging task?
   Yes ☐   No ☐

If you answered "yes" to one or more questions in this section, you may be dealing with issues of anxiety, fear, worry and doubt.

SECTION #7:

25) Are you sad when you see others attain achievements that you have not?
   Yes ☐   No ☐

26) Do you want things that you see others have?
   Yes ☐   No ☐

27) Do you dislike complimenting others on their victories?
   Yes ☐   No ☐

28) Are you judgmental or critical of others?
   Yes ☐   No ☐

If you answered "yes" to one or more of the questions in this section, you may be dealing with the issue of jealousy.

Section #8:

29) Do you not take criticism well?

Yes ☐   No ☐

30) Do you feel negative emotions when others tell you what to do?

Yes ☐   No ☐

31) Do you dislike accepting change?

Yes ☐   No ☐

32) Do you like to always get your way?

Yes ☐   No ☐

If you answered "yes" to one or more of the questions in this section, you may be dealing with the issue of stubbornness.

Section #9:

33) Do you passionately dislike others around you?

Yes ☐   No ☐

34) Do you wish to harm the people who have done you wrong?

Yes ☐   No ☐

35) Do you dislike certain ethnic groups or certain types of people?

Yes ☐   No ☐

36) Would you murder someone if there were no consequences behind it?

Yes ☐   No ☐

37) Do you think you are better than some people?

Yes ☐   No ☐

38) Would you consider yourself to be more fortunate than others?
Yes ☐   No ☐

39) Do you judge others around you?
Yes ☐   No ☐

40) Do you dislike dealing with people who you believe are not on your level?
Yes ☐   No ☐

If you answered "yes" to one or more of the questions in this section, you may be dealing with issues of pride and arrogance.

SECTION #10:

41) Do you tell lies when it is convenient?
Yes ☐   No ☐

42) Do you make promises that you often break?
Yes ☐   No ☐

43) Do you use words loosely to appease others around you?
Yes ☐   No ☐

44) Do you at times pretend to be someone other than who you are?
Yes ☐   No ☐

If you answered "yes" to one or more of the questions, you may be dealing with issues of deceit and untrustworthiness.

SECTION #11:

45) Do you dislike sharing what you have with others?
Yes ☐   No ☐

46) Do you keep to yourself knowledge that can benefit others?
Yes ☐   No ☐

47) Are you selfish with your possessions?
Yes ☐   No ☐

48) Are you afraid to teach others what you know because they may surpass you?
Yes ☐   No ☐

If you answered "yes" to one or more of those questions in this section, you may be dealing with issues of jealousy and insecurity.

SECTION 12:

49) Do you act before considering the effects your actions may have on others?
Yes ☐   No ☐

50) Is your life all about you and what you can get?
Yes ☐   No ☐

51) Will you jeopardize others so you can advance?
Yes ☐   No ☐

52) Do you care about what others do, say or feel?
Yes ☐   No ☐

If you answered "yes" to one or more of these questions in this section, you may be dealing with issues of self-centeredness and selfish ambition.

SECTION #13:

53) When people say things that you don't like, are you unable to stay quiet?

Yes ☐   No ☐

54) When you feel negative emotions such as anger or resentment, do you automatically react?
Yes ☐   No ☐

55) Are you quick to use your fists to handle problems?
Yes ☐   No ☐

56) Do you wear your feelings on your sleeve, so that it is easy to tell how you feel?
Yes ☐   No ☐

If you answered "yes" to any of the questions in this section, you may be dealing with issues of rage and anger.

Now that you have answered the questions, go back and review all the yes boxes you checked and check off the areas in the chart below that you may need to work on according to your answers.

AREAS OF WEAKNESS GRID
___Shame and Guilt – Section 1
___Self-pity and low self-esteem – Section 2
___Anger, Resentment, and Unforgiveness – Section 3
___Depression and Frustration – Section 4
___Codependency and insecurity – Section 5
___Anxiety, Fear, Worry and Doubt – Section 6
___Jealousy – Section 7
___Stubbornness – Section 8
___Pride and Arrogance – Section 9
___Deceit and Untrustworthiness – Section 10
___Jealousy and Insecurity – Section 11
___Self-centeredness and Selfish-ambition –Section 12
___Rage and Anger – Section 13

Throughout the *Voices of Consequence Series*, we will work on improving our areas of weakness. Do not be dismayed! Help is on the way! Congratulations for stepping out of the darkness of denial and getting ready to step into the brightness of enlightenment!

Instructions: Read the questions below carefully. Then, check the box "yes" or "no," according to which answer best describes your actions.

Moral Inventory of Good Character Traits

SECTION #1:

1) Do you give to others or help them with no expectations in return?
   Yes ☐   No ☐

2) Do you treat others just as well as you treat yourself?
   Yes ☐   No ☐

3) Do you naturally have an interest in the well-being of others?
   Yes ☐   No ☐

SECTION #2:

4) Do you make it a principle to always tell the truth?
   Yes ☐   No ☐

5) Do you avoid situations where you may have to compromise your integrity to appease others?
   Yes ☐   No ☐

6) Do you value the words you tell others and stand by them?
   Yes ☐   No ☐

SECTION #3:

7) Are you faithful to others when you make commitments?
   Yes ☐   No ☐

8) Do you protect your friends from slander or destruction at all costs?
Yes ☐   No ☐

9) Are you there for others whom you love during both good times and bad times?
Yes ☐   No ☐

SECTION #4:

10) Are you modest when you are around others, treating people equally even if your achievements in life are more substantial than theirs?
Yes ☐   No ☐

11) Do you acknowledge God as the Source of all good things in your life?
Yes ☐   No ☐

12) Are you grateful for all that you have, even during difficult times?
Yes ☐   No ☐

SECTION #5:

13) Do you make it a principle to find ways to give back to others?
Yes ☐   No ☐

14) When you see someone in need, do you extend a helping hand?
Yes ☐   No ☐

15) Do you teach others the skill sets and talents you have learned?
Yes ☐   No ☐

SECTION #6:

16) Do you make it a policy to count your blessings on a regular basis?
Yes ☐   No ☐

17) Are you generally pleasant and kind to others?
Yes ☐   No ☐

18) Do you remain positive even when circumstances around you may seem negative?
Yes ☐   No ☐

SECTION #7:

19) Can you be counted on to perform the tasks and duties you have committed to?
Yes ☐   No ☐

20) Do you take your promises seriously?
Yes ☐   No ☐

21) Are you consistent in your performance and complete the task that you begin?
Yes ☐   No ☐

SECTION #8:

22) Do you wait patiently for your expected results?
Yes ☐   No ☐

23) Is it easy for you to deal with others even when they are irrational?
Yes ☐   No ☐

24) Are you able to pass up an urge if it is not the right time to fulfill it?
Yes ☐   No ☐

25) Do you treat others well even if they are not nice to you?
Yes ☐   No ☐

26) Do you share positive words with others whom you encounter?
Yes ☐   No ☐

27) Do you do good things to people with no expectancy of return?
Yes ☐   No ☐

SECTION 10:

28) When others injure you, are you able to control your temper?
Yes ☐   No ☐

29) Do you think about the consequences of your actions before you act?
Yes ☐   No ☐

30) Do you try to rid yourself of negative thoughts when they creep in?
Yes ☐   No ☐

SECTION #11:

31) Do you make it a policy to keep positive thoughts in your mind even during adversity?
Yes ☐   No ☐

32) Do you prefer a calm, tranquil environment?
Yes ☐   No ☐

33) Do you encourage those around you to get along and to consider the needs of others?
Yes ☐   No ☐

SECTION 12:

34) Do you easily forgive others who have wronged you?
Yes ☐   No ☐

35) Do you pray for your enemies and wish them the best?
Yes ☐   No ☐

36) Are you compassionate toward others who have made mistakes and experienced hardships?

Yes ☐   No ☐

Now that you are finished answering the questions, go back and review all the boxes you checked "yes" to, and check off the areas in the chart below that describe your good attributes according to your answers.

AREAS OF STRENGTH GRID

___Loving/Kind – Section 1

___Honest/Truthful – Section 2

___Loyal/Faithful – Section 3

___Humble/Content –Section 4

___Generous/Helpful – Section 5

___Joyous/Positive – Section 6

___Trustworthy/Dependable – Section 7

___Patient/Calm – Section 8

___Kind/Compassionate – Section 9

___Self-controlled/Temperate – Section 10

___Peaceful/Peacemaker – Section 11

___Merciful/Forgiving- Section 12

BAD RELATIONSHIPS INVENTORY LIST

1) Do you closely associate with people who continuously criticize you and tear down your ideas or your comments?

Yes ☐   No ☐

If yes, please list their names below:

_____

_____

_____

_____

_____

2) Do you closely associate with people who struggle with or resist complimenting you or your achievements, or on other parts of your life?

Yes ☐   No ☐

If yes, please list their names below:

_____

_____

_____

_____

_____

_____

_____

3) Do you closely associate with people who distract you from being productive?

Yes ☐   No ☐

If yes, please list their names below:

_____

_____

_____

_____

4) Do you closely associate with people who tend to lead you into trouble?

Yes ☐   No ☐

If yes, please list their names below:

_____

_____

_____

_____

5) Do you closely associate with others who always seem to have a problem and who burden you with their troubles and mishaps?

Yes ☐   No ☐

If yes, please list their names below:

_____

_____

_____

_____

6) Do you closely associate with others whose general conversation is about negative and unproductive topics?
Yes ☐   No ☐

   If yes, please list their names below:

   _____

   _____

   _____

   _____

7) Do you closely associate with people who constantly talk negatively about others and who degrade people to make themselves look better?
Yes ☐   No ☐

   If yes, please list their names below:

   _____

   _____

   _____

   _____

8) Do you closely associate with people who always seem to need something from you, who always take and seldom give?
Yes ☐   No ☐

If yes, please list their names below:

_____

_____

_____

_____

If you answered "yes" to any one of these questions, write down the names of the people you recorded in your answer chart below. Also list how many answers their names appeared in.

BAD RELATIONSHIPS GRID

Names of People   The number of lists they are on

_____

_____

_____

_____

_____

_____

_____

_____

_____

_____

_____

_____

_____

_____

_____

_____

_____

_____

_____

Examine the names on the bad relationships list and begin to make arrangements to detach from these people as soon as possible. Your relationship with these people may hinder your future and cause you undue hardships.

Chapter Questions

1) Why is denial dangerous?

_____

_____

_____

_____

2) Why do bad character traits cause our lives to stagnate?

_____

_____

_____

_____

3) List some bad character traits.

_____

_____

_____

_____

4) List some good character traits.

_____

_____

_____

_____

5) Why is it dangerous to associate with negative people?

_____

_____

_____

_____

Writing Assignment- Journal Entry #4

Write a list of the personal weaknesses you have discovered while completing your moral inventory. Discuss how each of these characteristics led to your imprisonment. Detail what negative behavioral patterns you developed as a result of each weakness. Explain how you will improve your overall "self" in order not to repeat the same mistakes.

_____

_____

_____

_____

_____

_____

_____

_____

_____

_____

_____

_____

_____

_____

_____

_____

_____

_____

_____

_____

_____

_____

_____

_____

_____

_____

_____

_____

_____

_____

_____

_____

_____

_____

_____

_____

_____

_____

_____

_____

_____

_____

_____

Chapter 5 Review

Accepting Responsibility for Our Actions

Along with acknowledging our shortcomings, we must also recognize our own wrong behavioral patterns. Many of us have spent years blaming others for our wrongdoings. As a result, we have blocked the pathway to change. Change can't occur until we admit there is a problem. In order to advance in life, we must be willing to accept personal responsibility for our wrong actions and not blame others for them.

Accepting responsibility for our actions occurs when we feel remorse for our wrongdoings and desire to change our course of action. We cannot become truly remorseful until we understand fully the effects our harmful behavior has had on our victims.

Many of us have been so self-centered that we have stayed trapped in the "woe is me" syndrome and have not accurately understood the effects our behavior has had on others. In all crimes, there is a victim. Often we are so engrossed with self-gain that we forget those whom we used as pawns and whom we victimized to obtain our goals.

It is time to accurately review our actions and to acknowledge all those who suffered as a result of our conduct.

Many of us have family members who have been left behind to grieve because of our actions. Some of us have children who look up to us, whom we've greatly let down and disappointed. It is imperative that we no longer just think about ourselves, but also that we consider our loved ones before we make decisions. We must accurately weigh the consequences of our actions and take into account all the parties who will be affected by them.

When we sow bad seeds by doing negative things, negativity is what we reap! Therefore, if we hurt others knowingly, or even unknowingly, we set the stage for hurt to come back to us. Let's break this negative cycle by becoming conscious of our choices and the effects of our actions on others!

Let's use this time to accurately analyze the effects our crimes have had on others. Let's ask ourselves: "Would I want someone to do the same thing to me?" Let's review the price we've had to pay for what we thought was an advancement or a shortcut, then measure the cost by answering the question, "Was it worth it?" As we are able to analyze the effects of our crimes on ourselves and on others, we position ourselves to truly become remorseful for our misdoings and to accept responsibility for our actions.

Accepting responsibility is a mature choice! It means no longer running away from or avoiding our real issues. It is exposing our weaknesses and wrong behavioral patterns, and then doing something about them. When we truly take responsibility for what we have done, we open the door for great changes. We no longer hold onto self-centered ways. Instead, we consider others, and we do not jeopardize the well-being of another for our own selfish gain. We think before we act, and we consider the consequences of our actions. We become better people!

Chapter Questions

1) After reading the three examples in the text, do you view the effects of your crime differently? Why or why not?

_____

_____

_____

_____

2) What is the difference between acknowledging your shortcomings and your acceptance of responsibility?

_____

_____

_____

_____

3) Why is it necessary to accept responsibility for our adverse actions?

_____

_____

_____

_____

4) Now that you have viewed your crime from a victim's standpoint, would you be reluctant to commit the same crime again? Why or why not?

_____

_____

_____

_____

5) How do you feel now that you have accepted responsibility for your actions?

_____

_____

_____

_____

6) In example 1 in the text, why did Maria feel like trafficking drugs was not wrong before she came into contact with Sandra?

_____

_____

_____

_____

7) In example 1 in the text, what made Maria open her eyes to the effects of her wrongdoings?

_____

_____

_____

_____

8) In example 2 in the text , what were the main reasons why Keisha got caught up in a lifestyle of crime?

_____

_____

_____

_____

9) In example 2 in the text , what opened Keisha's eyes to the effects of her wrongdoings?

_____

_____

_____

_____

10) In example 2 in the text , was Keisha also victimized by Ann? If so, would it be easy for Keisha to block her own wrongdoings by magnifying what was done to her? Why or why not?

_____

_____

_____

_____

11) In example 3 in the text , why was Debbie vulnerable to influences compelling her to join a gang?

_____

_____

_____

_____

12) In example 3 in the text , how did the woman change Debbie's perspective about her crime?

_____

_____

_____

_____

_____

Writing Assignment- Journal Entry #5

Write a letter to one of the victims of your crime, which may include a family member or loved one. Ask them for forgiveness, and clearly state the actions you took that were wrong. Explain to them how you acknowledge their pain as a result of those actions, and outline for the victims what you are actively doing to permanently change your former ways.

_____

_____

_____

_____

_____

_____

_____

_____

_____

_____

_____

_____

_____

_____

_____

_____

_____

_____

_____

_____

_____

_____

_____

_____

_____

_____

_____

_____

_____

_____

_____

_____

_____

_____

_____

_____

CHAPTER 6 REVIEW

Closing the Doors to Shame and Guilt

In the last chapter, we began to uncover the adverse behavior that led to our incarceration, and we dealt with the effects our crimes have had on others. This discovery allowed us to accurately view our actions, creating remorse for our wrong behavior, which in turn led to acceptance of personal responsibility.

It is important that we do not hold on to feelings of shame and guilt arising from our past actions. Now that we have realized the roots of our difficulties and have found avenues to correct the behavior that followed, it's time to release all feelings of guilt and shame!

In God's eyes, yesterday no longer counts. When we confess our shortcomings and acknowledge our wrongdoings, God forgives us and no longer remembers our past. Therefore, yesterday's setbacks can no longer hinder us. Today, we start with a clean slate!

There can be no progress if we handcuff ourselves to the past, so we have no choice but to release it. Everything that happened had a purpose. Our endurance has made us stronger, wiser individuals. Our hardships have given us compassion for others who also have experienced similar setbacks. It is our victory testimony that will inspire others to also push through their storm.

The very thing we regret most, or are shameful of in the present, will be what God uses to demonstrate His power to others. At this moment we may be unable to see the purpose in our pain and our difficult experiences, but it is all working together for God's great purpose for our lives. The reward will far exceed the suffering. The key is patience and endurance.

When we are able to see our hardships from God's perspective, we can endure. There is no reason to hold onto feelings of shame, guilt, or regret. Everything happened just as it was intended. It led you to this place where you will now discover your purpose – which is the reason God put you on this Earth!

Shame comes from the thought of being wrong or inadequate. It is a sense of worthlessness that can turn into self-pity.

When we feel ashamed, we lose our self-esteem and our self-worth, which is dangerous because it causes us to stagnate and lose the faith we need to progress. Shame creates a desire to hide and move away from others so that our inadequacies won't be revealed. We cannot move forward when shame causes us to run away or stay back in the shadows. The only way to soar is to rid ourselves of shame!

Guilt is the remorseful feeling we get when we know that we did something that was unethical or wrong. It is the emotion God gives us to signal that we have moved off track. Once we detect guilt, we must address our wrong actions, then immediately discard this emotion. Holding on to guilt can be deadly. Guilty feelings lead to serious depression, suicidal thoughts, and other self-destructive emotions.

We all make mistakes, so it's okay to feel guilty when we do something wrong. Guilt at that point is our signal to correct our behavior. When we feel that emotion, we must analyze what we have done to create this reaction, then address the issue , discard the guilt, and move on!

In the last chapter we addressed the importance of our acceptance of responsibility. We were able to view our crimes from the correct perspective, causing us to feel shame, regret, and guilt. These feelings were necessary in order for us to sincerely change our course of life, but they must not be retained.

The guilty subconscious demands punishment for negative actions. It causes us to self-impose unhappiness, depression, unworthiness, and even physical damage. Guilt causes us to feel as though we deserve to be constantly punished, so we beat ourselves down instead of lifting ourselves up. We settle for less, and let others treat us harshly, because deep down inside we feel we don't deserve anything better. This can become self-destructive because our minds become programmed for failure! As a result, failure is what comes our way!

The only way to soar in life is to rid ourselves of shame and guilt. We accomplish this through self-forgiveness. Self-forgiveness is the act of learning from our past while being conscious of our inherent goodness in the present. It is the heart of our healing process. It is the only instrument we can use to ensure that we move ahead and not make the same mistakes again. Self-forgiveness creates and restores our self-worth and self-esteem, and gives us the will power we need to move on.

True self-forgiveness requires courage and honesty. It is not redefining an offense as non-offensive or down-playing our adverse actions. It is to evaluate the truth of what occurred and to reposition ourselves not to take the same course, while at the same time allowing ourselves a clear conscience to move ahead with a positive mindset.

The key action that is necessary to complete the process of self-forgiveness is becoming aligned with "self." As we align with "self," we awaken to wisdom and compassion, which we need to help us make better conscious choices. Better choices enable us to increase our self-respect and give us a healthy sense of responsibility towards ourselves and others. Better choices also increase our courage and belief in "self," which is necessary to pursue our dreams and goals. Our alignment with "self" helps us forgive ourselves.

The purpose of self-forgiveness is to shine light on our fears and the destructive judgments that have kept us bound. In many cases, we have been our own jailer, holding ourselves in a self-made prison. Self-forgiveness is the challenge of being accountable and learning to know, accept, and love ourselves despite our adverse past experiences. It is the formula that separates us from our past and propels us into the future!

Chapter Questions

1) What is guilt?

_____

_____

_____

_____

2) What is shame?

_____

_____

_____

_____

3) Why are guilt and shame toxic to our emotional health?

_____

_____

_____

_____

4) How do we rid ourselves of guilt and shame?

_____

_____

_____

_____

5) What is self-forgiveness?

_____

_____

_____

_____

6) Why is it easy to get trapped in guilt and shame when in prison?

_____

_____

_____

_____

7) How does God view our past actions?

_____

_____

_____

_____

8) What is the goal of the enemy in constantly sending us thoughts of guilt, shame and regret?

_____

_____

_____

_____

9) How do we come into alignment with "self?"

_____

_____

_____

_____

10) How do we deal with others who try to keep bringing up our past actions?

_____

_____

_____

_____

Example

Jaime grew up in a good family in Memphis, Tennessee. Her parents were strict and required Jaime to work hard and get good grades. All was well with Jamie as a little girl, but when she reached high school, she got a taste of freedom and rebelled against her parent's strict ways.

Jaime's rebellious behavior caused her parents to become even stricter, so she was constantly being punished. Jaime finally had enough, and one day she packed everything she owned and left home.

At first, Jaime stayed with a friend. Then she decided to move in with an older man whom she'd met who lived in Georgia. The man abused drugs and influenced Jaime to do the same.

Jaime got hooked. She turned to prostitution to support her habit. Jaime hated her lifestyle, but she was in too deep to turn back.

One day, Jaime went to the OB/GYN when she discovered an unusual swelling in her vaginal area. At her doctor's visit, she discovered she had contracted herpes. Frightened by her diagnosis and her potential contraction of another venereal disease, she chose to quit prostitution and instead deal drugs to support her habit.

All was well, or Jaime so thought, until her supplier received a federal indictment and started snitching on those under him in order to reduce his time. Jaime was set-up by her boss through a wiretap and was charged with distribution. As a result, she was sentenced to a mandatory minimum of 10 years in federal prison.

Jaime was scared and confused in her new prison environment. She had no support there, but shame and guilt caused her not to reach out to her parents, whom she hadn't spoken to or seen in over 5 years.

Jaime wasn't gay, but she decided to become involved with a girl named Rebecca so that she could have the things she needed in prison. Rebecca had strong family support, so she was able to take care of Jaime. Rebecca gave Jaime both attention and time, and Jaime quickly fell in love with Rebecca. As time passed, Rebecca became very jealous and abusive. She realized her control over Jaime and took advantage of it. Jaime allowed it, believing that this was what she deserved.

As Jaime allowed Rebecca to abuse her, Rebecca lost interest in Jaime. Gaining Jamie's love was no longer a challenge, and Rebecca became bored. Jaime had a friend, Terry, who was from the same hometown as Jaime and was at the same county jail with Jaime when she'd awaited sentencing. The two girls became good friends, and Jaime embraced Terry, who came to prison well after Jaime. Like Jaime, Terry had little money and no family support. She envied the ease Jaime had in making ends meet.

Jaime introduced Terry to Rebecca, and one day the two of them announced to Jaime that they were going to be a couple. Jaime was devastated! She felt like her life was over. Everything bad that ever happened to her kept playing over and over in her mind. She began to experience feelings of guilt and shame. As those emotions overtook her, she tried to commit suicide.

In the hospital ward of the prison, Jaime was introduced to the chaplain, who suggested Jaime reconcile with her parents. Jaime was reluctant at first because she was afraid and ashamed of all the wrong she knew she had done. However, she took the chaplain's advice and summoned the strength to call her parents.

To Jaime's surprise, her parents were happy to hear from her. They'd feared Jamie had been abducted and was possibly dead. They rushed to the prison to see her and rekindled their relationship.

Within a year, Jaime's mother had found a good attorney who discovered a loophole in the government's case. He argued the disparity of Jaime's sentence as compared to her boss, who had gotten a 3-year sentence because of his cooperation with the government. The argument made it to the appellate court, where Jaime's sentence was reduced to the same 3-year sentence as her boss had received.

Jaime's new chance at life sparked a change in her. She is currently living at home with her parents while attending college. She has learned from her past and is now determined to only look ahead!

1) What kept Jaime from reaching out to her parents?

_____

_____

_____

_____

2) Why did Jaime think it was okay for Rebecca to abuse her?

_____

_____

_____

_____

3) What event led to Jaime's attempt to commit suicide?

_____

_____

_____

_____

4) Why did Jaime feel as though she wasn't worthy of living?

_____

_____

_____

_____

5) How did Jaime's life change when she dealt with her fear and contacted her parents? Was it what she expected?

_____

_____

_____

_____

Writing Assignment- Journal Entry #6

Write down the events that have caused you the most shame and guilt. Then list what you can do to fix each situation. If you cannot remedy the problem, write: "There is nothing I can do to fix the situation." Describe what you will do to ensure a better future and how you will not repeat the same mistakes. These actions will be a part of your written plans for a greater future.

_____

_____

_____

_____

_____

_____

_____

_____

_____

_____

_____

_____

_____

_____

_____

_____

_____

_____

_____

_____

_____

_____

_____

_____

_____

_____

_____

_____

_____

_____

_____

_____

_____

_____

_____

_____

_____

_____

_____

_____

_____

_____

CHAPTER 7 REVIEW
Forgiving Others Who Have Wronged Us

The root of most offender behavior is unhealed anger, rage, grief, guilt, and shame from childhood issues. Many of us have suffered physical or emotional abuse as a child that significantly influenced who we have become.

It is important that we correctly deal with the pain which has been inflicted upon us. When we hold onto anger, bitterness, and resentment, we halt our ability to grow emotionally and spiritually and become handcuffed to our past. We must not carry around the baggage of being a victim. It is important to deal with the emotions of hurt, pain, and betrayal, so that we will no longer remain a victim. The way that we release our hurt and our pain is to forgive.

Forgiveness becomes easier when we view the actions of others from the correct perspective. We discussed previously that we all have an enemy whose job is to steal, kill, and destroy. He works intensely to distract us from discovering our purpose. He uses others who have weak minds and who are ignorant of his works. He floods their minds with negative thoughts and uses them to inflict harm on others. Many act out on behalf of the enemy unknowingly and cause great pain to others. This is not an excuse for their wrong actions, but it is important for us to realize who our true enemy is.

It is vital that we know God will not forgive us unless we forgive others who have hurt us. Regardless of what a person has done to us, we must forgive them. Forgiving them doesn't excuse their actions, but it does rid us of inner turmoil.

One of the greatest mistakes we can make in life is to try to avenge ourselves. We now have the help of our "Higher Power" and whatever our problems or concerns, we can take them to God in prayer. When we turn over to God those who have harmed us, He has a way of dealing with them that reflects His strength. Many of us are confused, believing that we are doing our abusers a favor when we forgive them. Forgiveness is not for them, it is for us! The longer we remain held captive in resentment and bitterness, the longer before we can move forward. We must do ourselves a favor and forgive all who caused us ill, regardless of what they have done. If not, we become shackled to the emotional pain and distress caused by unforgiveness. When we choose to forgive, we are able to experience relief.

Unforgiveness is deadly. It produces a root of bitterness that poisons our entire body. Many people have died of diseases that stemmed from unforgiveness. Harboring resentment and bitterness is a form of bondage. It holds us captive to the ill will of others, which becomes self-imprisonment. When we don't forgive, we yield our lives over to the control of another person.

Forgiveness is an act of self-interest. We forgive so we won't allow our emotions to be fueled by someone else's ignorance, fears, and problems. When we decide to forgive, we restore our power, making forgiveness a pathway to our self-empowerment.

Forgiveness is not pretending or ignoring our true feelings. It is not acting as though all is well. Forgiveness doesn't mean you approve or support the behavior of the person who caused you pain. It also doesn't mean that you should hesitate to take actions needed to change your situation. You do not have to associate with or befriend your abuser. Forgiveness means you simply detach from all hateful feelings and anger toward the person who has harmed you.

Forgiveness is not forgetting an act; it is forgetting the negative emotions that keep you bound by the act. When you truly forgive a person who has hurt you, you can remember what they have done, but you are no longer controlled or ruled by their actions. In other words, to forgive is not to forgive the act that was done, it is instead to forgive the person who has done it.

Forgiveness brings peace and restoration into our lives. As we forgive, we release the shackles of the past and allow ourselves the positive energy we need to move forward in life.

Chapter Questions

1) What is forgiveness?

_____

_____

_____

_____

2) What is unforgiveness?

_____

_____

_____

_____

3) Why are people so reluctant to forgive others?

_____

_____

_____

_____

4) Why is unforgiveness dangerous?

_____

_____

_____

_____

5) What misconceptions do people have of what must be done in order to forgive?

_____

_____

_____

_____

6) What is God's requirement concerning forgiveness?

_____

_____

_____

_____

7) How does unforgiveness affect our relationship with God?

_____

_____

_____

_____

8) Is forgiveness given for the person who abuses us or for ourselves? Why or why not?

_____

_____

_____

_____

9) Why are our abusers also considered "victims"?

_____

_____

_____

_____

10) What is the proper way to deal with a person who has harmed you?

_____

_____

_____

_____

Example: The Wrong Way to Forgive

Sheritta began dating a man named Charlie whom she loved greatly. Charlie and Sheritta's relationship became very serious, so they decided to move in together.

Several months passed and Sheritta noticed Charlie was becoming very jealous and possessive. One night her cousin Bobby asked Sheritta for a ride to the store. Charlie had never met Bobby; so when Bobby arrived at the house, Charlie had no clue he was Sheritta's cousin. Charlie became furious and lost his self-control. Without asking questions, Charlie assaulted Bobby and the two exchanged blows. When Sheritta tried to stop the fight and to explain to Charlie who Bobby was, Charlie began to hit Sheritta.

Sheritta ended up with a broken nose and a black eye. When Charlie finally calmed down, Sheritta was able to explain to him that Bobby was only her cousin. Charlie felt very remorseful for his actions and sincerely apologized. He took Sheritta out to dinner and sent roses to her at her place of employment, 3 days in a row. Sheritta forgave him and the two continued to live together.

About a month later, Charlie wrongly suspected Sheritta of sleeping with her college professor. He began to stalk Sheritta, following her without her knowledge.

Sheritta's term paper was due, and she was going to be late handing it in. She asked her professor if she could have an extension, and he agreed. The professor was teaching a night class at a local community college, and he asked Sheritta to drop the paper off to him there.

Charlie followed Sheritta to the local community class, where she coincidentally pulled up in the parking lot at the same time as the professor. When the two of them got out of the car to meet each other, Charlie felt that was enough to prove Sheritta's disloyalty. Charlie ferociously leapt from the car and began to beat the professor. He then choked Sheritta until she lost consciousness.

Today Sheritta suffers from brain damage because of her injury.

1) Why was Sheritta easily able to forgive Charlie?

_____

_____

_____

_____

2) Why was Sheritta's method of forgiveness dangerous?

_____

_____

_____

_____

3) What would have been the correct way for Sheritta to forgive Charlie?

_____

_____

_____

_____

4) Who else suffered because of Sheritta not adequately caring for self? Is that fair? Why or why not?

_____

_____

_____

_____

5) What happened to Sheritta as a result of her wrong choices?

_____

_____

_____

_____

Note: After Charlie beat Sheritta the first time, she had the option of protecting herself by detaching from him. The detachment didn't have to be nasty or unloving. It was simply a gesture to save herself from further harm. Sheritta could still have forgiven Charlie by not holding resentment or ill will toward him, while caring for "self" by departing. Instead she opted to forgive, forget, and stay. She took no preventive measures to protect herself. As a result, she was harmed again!

ABUSERS CHART

List the names of those who have hurt you in the past.	Summarize what they did to you in a sentence.

Writing Assignment- Journal Entry #7

Write a letter to the person(s) who harmed you the most. Tell them how their actions have affected you and how they made you feel. Recount the moment by expressing it on paper. Release all of your feelings. Then close the letter by informing the person(s) that you forgive them. From the teachings, detail the ways in which they are also a victim of the enemy. Convince your abuser(s) to open their eyes and encourage them to change their ways.

Note: You do not have to give this letter to the person(s) unless you so choose. This letter is for you to let go of what's trapped inside. Let this be the last and final time you take yourself through this emotional process. Write it all down and then release your feelings by forgiving your abusers.

_____

_____

_____

_____

_____

_____

_____

_____

_____

_____

_____

_____

_____

_____

CHAPTER 8 REVIEW

Changing Our "Stinking Thinking"

Many of us have landed in various adverse positions in life based on our impaired thinking. Our accumulated thoughts form our beliefs, and our beliefs allow us to make certain judgments and choices. Everything we do first starts as a thought. Our thoughts forge our actions; therefore, it is important that we learn to control our thoughts. As we rearrange our thoughts, we automatically rearrange our lives.

The root of our problems stems from wrong thinking that we have assimilated from others, which is called our "stinking thinking." In order to take charge over our destiny and to overcome adversity, we must break our negative thinking patterns.

To understand the importance of our thinking we must comprehend the law of attraction. The law of attraction is a universal law that states: "Like attracts like." This means that, as you think a thought, you are also attracting such like thoughts to you. Thus, whatever thoughts we have been consumed with have resulted in our current experience. Essentially, our thoughts have radiated into the atmosphere and brought us back more of what we have been thinking about. In order to break the chains of adversity, we must change the signals in our minds from negative to positive thoughts. As we think positive thoughts, we will become consumed with positive experiences. Changing our lives is as simple as changing our thinking patterns.

Our goal in the *Voices of Consequences Series* is to pull down the strongholds of "stinking thinking" and replace them with healthy thinking. In order to be productive, continuously sustaining a positive mindset must become a way of life. As we become governed by proper thinking, we rid ourselves of the negativity that has plagued us.

According to the law of attraction, the only reason people do not have what they want is because they are thinking about the wrong things. They are focused more on what they don't want rather than what they do want. When we allow ourselves to experience depressing thoughts of defeat, worry and doubt, they become the basis of our existence. The more we focus on these thoughts, the stronger their negative impact is on our lives. That is why we must rid ourselves of negative thoughts as quickly as we detect them.

Our emotions are our indicators. They let us know what we are consciously and subconsciously thinking. When we are feeling disturbed or bothered, that is our signal to change our thoughts. It is detrimental to our well-being if our minds wallow in negative thoughts; if we allow this practice, negativity is sure to follow. Our lives will become chaotic because of the negative thinking we allowed to take root.

We combat our "stinking thinking" when we have the right perspective about our circumstances. Regardless of what our current experience is, we must train ourselves to recognize the good that will come from it. When we are able to discover the good in all things, it brings us hope, and our hope develops into joy. When we detect the good, we begin to experience positive thoughts that are transmitted into the universe, bringing us back more good experiences. As we change our perspective, which is ultimately changing our thoughts, we also change our experience. Instantly, our bad situation is no longer bad because we have identified the good in it. Our new perspective sheds light on the bright light at the end of the tunnel, and our experiences become bearable.

In order to change our lives we must become conscious of our thinking. The Bible instructs us in Philippians, Chapter 4, verse 8, "Whatever things are noble, whatever things are just, whatever things are pure, whatever things are lovely, whatever things are of good report, if there is any virtue and if there is any praise – meditate on these things."

As we make a concentrated effort to think about the good, positive, and healthy, positive results will develop. The key to unlocking the prison doors lies within our minds! As a woman thinketh in her heart, so is she.

Our challenge in this journey will be to consciously become aware of our thoughts by using our feelings as indicators. When negativity tries to creep in, we must swiftly dethrone every unhappy thought by changing our perspective to seek the good in our lives. As we focus on the good, we shift our perspective and good ultimately becomes our experience!

Chapter Questions

1) What is "stinking thinking?"

_____

_____

_____

_____

2) How did we develop "stinking thinking?"

_____

_____

_____

_____

3) How can we now rid ourselves of our "stinking thinking?"

_____

_____

_____

_____

4) What is the law of attraction?

_____

_____

_____

_____

5) How do we bring about good experiences into our lives?

_____

_____

_____

_____

6) Why is it dangerous to dwell on thoughts of fear, worry and doubt?

_____

_____

_____

_____

7) What are the indicators to let us know we are experiencing negative thoughts?

_____

_____

_____

_____

8) Why is our perspective on how we view our circumstances important?

_____

_____

_____

_____

9) What happens if we don't take control over our thoughts?

_____

_____

_____

_____

10) What kind of thoughts should we be experiencing?

_____

_____

_____

_____

Chapter Example Questions

Read the example about Ladonna and Denise, in Chapter 8 in the text, and answer the following questions:

1) Denise and LaDonna grew up in the same household yet they turned out very differently? Why?

_____

_____

_____

_____

2) What made Denise believe gang life was cool?

_____

_____

_____

_____

3) Why did Denise feel as though her mother didn't love her? Was she correct? Why or why not?

_____

_____

_____

_____

4) What changed Denise's life?

_____

_____

_____

_____

5) Do you have any similarities in your old way of thinking to that of Denise's? Why or why not?

_____

_____

_____

_____

Writing Assignment- Journal Entry #8

Write down 10 negative thought patterns or misconceptions that you have developed in your lifetime. Then list the positive thoughts that you can now use to replace those negative thoughts.

_____

_____

_____

_____

_____

_____

_____

_____

_____

_____

_____

_____

_____

_____

_____

_____

_____

_____

_____

_____

_____

_____

_____

_____

_____

_____

_____

_____

_____

_____

_____

_____

_____

_____

_____

_____

_____

_____

_____

_____

CHAPTER 9 REVIEW
Managing Our Emotions

As human beings, we all have emotions. Emotions are our indicators that let us know how we should feel or react. They are the source of our joy, sadness, fear, and anger. Our emotions have been given to us to help guide us, but we are not to be ruled by them! Instead, we must acknowledge our feelings, assess the reasons behind them, and then rationally decide how we should react. Our job is to manage and monitor our emotions, instead of making rash decisions or reacting negatively.

Gaining control over our lives begins with learning to manage our emotions. Our real battle begins and ends within our minds! When we learn how to govern and control our mindset, we develop the skill set of managing our emotions. Mastering our thoughts is the key to mastering our emotions! This comes with diligence, time, and practice.

The emotions that we need to beware of are negative emotions, which include fear, worry, doubt, depression, anger, hatred, anxiety, shame, guilt, greed, jealousy, and revenge. When we harbor these emotions, we develop destructive behavior patterns as a result. Whatever thoughts we are consumed by dictate what we will ultimately become. If we allow ourselves to become filled with negative feelings and emotions, we will eventually act upon our thoughts, taking part in negativity. We remove these unproductive feelings and emotions by simply removing our negative thoughts. Cleansing our thoughts is done in a state of meditation. We meditate by closing our eyes and placing our minds in a peaceful state. As we become peaceful during mediation, we purposely rid ourselves of all oppressive ideas. We envision ourselves happy, healthy, and whole, and we experience the feelings that come with these positive emotions. As we disperse our negative thoughts, we instantly feel soothed and calm inside. We repeat this process each time such thoughts try to creep in. Meditation becomes our source of self-cleansing. Just as we need a daily bath to cleanse us of dirt and debris, we need to meditate daily to cleanse our minds of negative thoughts.

Dealing properly with anger is an overwhelming problem for many of us. The abuse we have had to endure has built up inside of us, causing us to become naturally angry people. When anger builds and we don't create a channel for it to be released, we suppress our anger. Suppressed anger is like a bomb waiting to explode. Many of us are walking bombshells. The smallest thing can trigger us into a rage.

Anger is a powerful emotion that can block other emotions. Anger can also block us from being able to clearly analyze the good that may come from our situations. Angry people generally view everything as negative. Anger dominates and overtakes our emotions until we address it properly.

Unresolved anger can turn into resentment. Resentment is the feeling of grievance or ill will towards another that lasts long after the original encounter. Unaddressed resentment eventually turns into hate, unforgiveness, and bitterness, which prevent us from receiving our blessings.

Anger should never be suppressed. We must allow ourselves to feel the emotion and take whatever action is necessary to protect ourselves. Then by all means, we must let it go! Anger will not just go away on its own, or by our ignoring it. All anger must be dealt with by releasing the energy that it carries. We can channel negative energy by practicing physical fitness, running, playing sports, writing about it, talking about it or by doing any other activities that require intense energy.

When rage arises, we must learn how to manage it by (a) allowing ourselves to feel the emotion and any underlying emotions, such as hurt or fear; (b) acknowledging our thoughts as they come, analyzing them to see if our understanding is correct; (c) talking over our feelings with someone we trust who is a positive person, getting their perspective on the situation; and (d) making a responsible decision about what actions we need to take to protect and care for "self," if any.

Another group of negative emotions that can affect us adversely are fear, worry, and doubt. These feelings can paralyze us. Fear of the unknown keeps us stuck in cycles with which we are uncomfortable. They paralyze us from venturing outside of familiar territories, making it hard to achieve our dreams.

The acronym for fear is: **F**alse **E**vidence **A**ppearing **R**eal. We must not fear anything or anyone, except God. When we make the correct choices in life, we are protected. God will always provide for us and keep us safe from hurt, harm, and danger. Therefore, fear should never be an option for us!

Fear is tormenting. When we allow it to come into our lives, we become flooded with more fearful events. Remember the law of attraction; whatever we think or believe, we attract more into our lives. That's why it is important to quickly discard fear.

A worried mind produces nothing worthwhile. It keeps us in a state of confusion and disbelief; thus, we will find it difficult to make proper decisions. When we are confused, we cannot operate at our fullest potential.

Worry is negative meditation. It is playing over and over in our minds the "What if?" As we ponder the negative thoughts associated with worrying, we send a command into the universe to bring us more of the very thing we are worried about. This is not good! Worrying produces nothing productive!

When we allow negative emotions to take root, such as fear, worry, and doubt, we are telling God we do not trust Him. We conquer these emotions by having faith and resting in the fact that we know our "Higher Power" has got our back!

We rid ourselves of all negative emotions by changing our thoughts. We must train our minds to believe that we are God's wonderful creation. As a result, we will receive God's best for our lives. Once we input positive thoughts into our minds, we will be able to function in peace and joy. It is this inner peace and joy that will direct the universe to send us an abundance of good.

Learning to manage our emotions is a process we can develop over time. We learn to discipline our thinking to control our reactions. The key is in what we feed our minds. As we make it a habit to fill ourselves with positive thoughts, controlling our emotions will become easy!

Chapter Questions

1) Why are our emotions important?

_____

_____

_____

_____

2) Why are our thoughts important?

_____

_____

_____

_____

3) Name 3 positive emotions and 3 negative emotions.

_____

_____

_____

_____

4) How do we manage our emotions?

_____

_____

_____

_____

5) How can anger be a positive motivator? How can it be a negative motivator?

_____

_____

_____

_____

6) How can we infuse positive emotions into our experiences?

_____

_____

_____

_____

7) What is the correct way to address issues when they arise?

_____

_____

_____

_____

8) What is the acronym for fear? Why is it a good description of fear?

_____

_____

_____

_____

9) Why is it not good to worry or doubt?

_____

_____

_____

_____

10) What do our actions tell God when we are fearful, worrisome or doubtful? Why?

_____

_____

_____

_____

Example

Sonja grew up in the inner city of Philadelphia, Pennsylvania. When Sonja turned seven years old her mother married her stepfather. Life changed dramatically for Sonja, who was accustomed to having her mother's time and attention all to herself.

Sonja's mother became pregnant a few years later and gave birth to Sonja's sister, Elaine. Sonja was always uncomfortable around her stepfather. Something about him gave her the creeps.

One day Sonja, at the age of 12, was home alone with her stepfather, and he did the unthinkable: He molested Sonja.

Sonja was afraid to tell anyone. She was scared about the consequences her stepfather said would happen if she did. She kept this deep, dark secret as he continued to molest Sonja on a regular basis for many years.

Sonja felt shameful and guilty about what was done to her. Deep down, she felt as if it was her fault, yet she was angry inside for the brutal way her stepfather treated her.

Sonja grew up without ever addressing the issue of her molestation. When she left home, Sonja felt like she was finally free from degradation.

However, Sonja became very defensive with men, especially in relationships. She built walls of protection, refusing to allow anyone to take advantage of her again. The smallest misstep would send Sonja into a rage! She would fight at the drop of a dime, especially if she thought someone was taking advantage of her.

One day, Sonja was in the grocery store shopping for food and a lady cut ahead of Sonja in line. When Sonja confronted the woman, she became became very rude and nasty, calling Sonja "ghetto trash." Sonja immediately reacted and began to beat the lady viciously with all the anger Sonja had roiling inside! Three males tried to pull Sonja away from the woman, but it was to no avail. Sonja's strength allowed her to severely injure this lady, whose husband turned out to be the town sheriff.

The cops were called to the scene, and Sonja was arrested and charged with aggravated assault. The lady's political influence gained Sonja a 5-year sentence in prison.

Sonja was devastated. She couldn't understand why so many punishing events had occurred. Inside, she wished she had never been born.

1) Why was Sonja so angry? What did her anger stem from?

_____

_____

_____

_____

2) How did Sonja take out her anger? Was this the correct way to deal with it? Why or why not?

_____

_____

_____

_____

3) Was Sonja a bad person? Why or why not?

_____

_____

_____

_____

4) Is there help for Sonja? How could she address her problems with anger?

_____

_____

_____

_____

5) How can Sonja work on healing from the wounds her stepfather inflicted?

_____

_____

_____

_____

Writing Assignment- Journal Entry #9

Keep a daily log of your feelings for one week. When you feel positive emotions, write them down and describe how you feel. Analyze why you are feeling this way. What happened to give you these emotions? Also, make a record of when you feel negative emotions. Write down the emotions and describe how you feel. Analyze what triggered these emotions. When you are finished, review your log and analyze how your emotions affect you. Then, list three ways you can diffuse your negative emotions and three ways you can sustain your positive emotions for longer periods of time.

_____

_____

_____

_____

_____

_____

_____

_____

_____

DAILY LOG OF EMOTIONS

Day	Emotions You Feel	Describe your feelings

1) What emotion did you feel most often?

_____

_____

_____

_____

2) How does that emotion make you feel?

_____

_____

_____

_____

3) What usually triggers that emotion?

_____

_____

_____

_____

4) How can you change or diffuse this emotion if it is a negative emotion?

_____

_____

_____

_____

5) How can you sustain this emotion if it is a positive emotion?

_____

_____

_____

_____

Writing Assignment Log

_____

_____

_____

_____

_____

_____

_____

_____

_____

_____

_____

_____

_____

_____

_____

_____

_____

_____

_____

_____

_____

_____

_____

_____

_____

_____

_____

_____

_____

_____

_____

_____

_____

_____

_____

CHAPTER 10 REVIEW
Learning to Care for "Self"

Many of us have spent years wearing masks, pretending to be other than who we are, in order to please those around us. Pretending has caused us to become out of alignment with "self." We have become so caught up in our roles of pleasing others that we don't know anymore what pleases "self." We spend our entire lives seeking to find someone whom we can please, with hopes that they will one day make us happy. This is a course of disillusionment! Happiness can only come from within! People, places, and things cannot bring us happiness.

Knowing that our source of joy comes from within, we must begin to work on our greatest asset, "self." We work on "self" by learning who we are and how to protect our best interest.

It's time to take pride in "self" and remove our masks. God created each of us to serve His divine purpose here on Earth. Each of us has special gifts, skill sets, and talents. It is up to us to go within and find them. Discovering our talents and our purpose is all a part of caring for "self."

We must regain our self-confidence. Without confidence we cannot achieve our goals and dreams. Self-confidence is generated as we begin to love, care, and nurture "self." As we do so, our faith in "self" increases along with our self-worth. In this season, we are to become our own lover, best friend and parent to "self" – loving ourselves unconditionally regardless of our faults. Taking on this role, we no longer wait for others to make us happy. We take control over our lives by creating our own self-happiness.

In our pursuit to care for "self," we must spend time analyzing "self" to determine our strengths and weaknesses, as well as what makes us happy or sad. As we become more in tune with our needs, we open the door to solutions. We work on our areas of weakness; we increase our areas of strength.

By caring for "self," we ultimately become better people who take pride in our well-being. We no longer allow others to impose on us, or to put us in harm's way. Instead we create boundaries, protecting ourselves from danger and from being taken advantage of by others.

Each day we wake up, we learn to take pride in "self." We compliment our "self" on our achievements and look for constant ways to improve. We learn how to properly care for our health by watching our diet and exercising daily. We also take the necessary time out to properly groom ourselves and take pride in our appearance.

As we care for "self," we send a signal out into the environment that tells others to show us the same level of respect that we have for our "self." In caring for our "self," we begin to feel good about our greatest asset, which is "self."

SELF-ANALYSIS CHART

1) What things do I like?
2) What do I dislike?

3) What brings me joy?

4) What actions do I take that make me feel good about "self?"

5) What are my favorite meals?

6) What are my favorite hobbies and activities?

7) What do I like to do to reward myself?

8) What are my favorite places?

9) What are my greatest fears?

10) What makes me feel sad or unsafe?

Chapter Questions

1) What is caring for "self?"

_____

_____

_____

_____

2) How do we care for "self?"

_____

_____

_____

_____

3) What are boundaries?

_____

_____

_____

_____

4) Why do we need boundaries to maintain healthy relationships?

_____

_____

_____

_____

5) Why is it important to maintain proper health and grooming, even in prison?

_____

_____

_____

_____

6) How do we get in alignment with "self" and our own needs?

_____

_____

_____

_____

7) Why is it easy to get caught up wearing masks representing other people?

_____

_____

_____

_____

8) Why is self-confidence vital?

_____

_____

_____

_____

9) Is taking care of "self" being selfish? Why or why not?

_____

_____

_____

_____

Writing Assignment- Journal Entry #10

From the self-analysis chart you created of your likes and dislikes, write an affirmation that details how you will begin to care for "self." Start off your affirmation as follows: "Today is a new day. Today I have learned the value of "self." I love and appreciate my "self," therefore I will....

_____

_____

_____

_____

_____

_____

_____

_____

_____

_____

_____

_____

_____

_____

_____

_____

_____

_____

_____

_____

_____

_____

_____

_____

_____

_____

_____

_____

_____

_____

_____

_____

_____

CHAPTER 11 REVIEW

Alternatives to Crime

There comes a point in our lives where we put away our childish ways and become more responsible in our choices. It is imperative that we recognize that all crimes come with consequences, either immediate or in the future. We can no longer jeopardize our future by continuing to commit crimes.

Many of use choose to live criminal lifestyles because we are seeking instant gratification. To achieve our goals, we decided to compromise and to skip necessary steps, allowing many of us to advance to the top. But, as quickly as we rose, we fell. Like a house being built, if we skip those steps and don't build a strong foundation, our house will always crumble. There are no exceptions! In order to live a victorious life, our new foundation must be built on strong ethical principles, composed of integrity mixed with hard work.

Being in prison, we have a lot of time to think about what we want to do in life. Now is the time to assess our skill sets and talents, and to determine how we can use them in a positive way.

A part of caring for "self" is self-analysis. We must identify the tasks we can do for an extensive period of time without becoming bored or tired. What do we do well? These are our gifts, talents, and skill sets.

When we tap into our talents and gifts, we must improve them. We can seek out a mentor, we can study and practice intensely in our areas of strength, making us grow and excel even further.

It's time to put together a plan! What can we do to make an honest living and enjoy doing at the same time? This is the exercise we do to tap into "self" and figure out how to become a "greater self."

There are many resources available to ex-felons. It is our job to seek them out, discover them, and utilize them. We must be ready to step down in order to step up. There are state and government funds that can help us in this journey. While we are in prison it is up to us to do the research and put together our plan of action.

Chapter Questions

1) Why must we give up our lifestyle of crime?

_____

_____

_____

_____

2) Why is it important to discover our skills and talents?

_____

_____

_____

_____

3) How can we overcome the stigma of being an ex-con?

_____

_____

_____

_____

4) In which ways do we discover more information about what field or occupation we wish to study, or the occupation we want to pursue?

_____

_____

_____

_____

5) Why are shortcuts dangerous?

_____

_____

_____

_____

Chapter Example Questions

Read the chapter examples in Chapter 11 in the text, and answer the following questions:

1) In example #1, how did the boys in the neighborhood use their talent for good?

_____

_____

_____

_____

2) What skill set did you utilize in the wrong way but which you can now use positively?

_____

_____

_____

_____

3) In example #2, why was DJ Clue able to excel beyond Baby Jay's achievements?

_____

_____

_____

_____

4) In example #2, what was DJ Clue's strategy?

_____

_____

_____

_____

5) In example #3, what disadvantages did Jessica have growing up?

_____

_____

_____

_____

6) In example #3, how did Jessica overcome her hurdle of poverty?

_____

_____

_____

_____

7) In example #3, how much time and work did it take for Jessica to reach her goal? Was it worth it in the end? Why or why not?

_____

_____

_____

_____

8) In example #4, what dilemma was Chrisilie faced with in the beginning of her life?

_____

_____

_____

_____

9) In example #4, how did Chrisilie defeat the odds and overcome her obstacles?

_____

_____

_____

_____

10) Name others you know who have overcome the stigma of being an ex-felon by becoming successful.

_____

_____

_____

_____

Writing Assignment- Journal Entry #11

Write down what you would like to pursue as an occupation after prison. Describe what steps you will have to take to accomplish this goal. Explain what you can do now in prison to prepare you for this experience.

_____

_____

_____

_____

_____

_____

_____

_____

_____

_____

_____

_____

_____

_____

_____

_____

_____

CHAPTER 12 REVIEW
Each Day Becoming a Better "Self"

Throughout our study of this book, we have learned strategies and techniques to restore our lives and become a better "self." It is important to maintain our progress. We must now implement these strategies and techniques into our everyday lives.

In this journey, we discovered our strengths and our weaknesses. With the results of our self-analysis, we can work diligently on improving our weaknesses while also improving our areas of strength. This will take hard work, diligence, and dedication. However, the results are well worth it!

We learned that the major battle in life is within our minds. Therefore, it is essential that we keep our minds cleansed and pure of negative thoughts and emotions.

When we wake up each day, before we get out of bed, it is essential that we change our atmosphere with our minds. We give thanks to God for the ability to see another day. Then we review in our minds all that we want to accomplish for that day. We walk through the expected events of that day, and we visualize ourselves accomplishing our tasks successfully. As we visualize our progress, we experience the feelings of success as if our experience was real. Our positive feelings affect the universe and bring us back more positive feelings. We purposely rid ourselves of negativity that may have slipped in from the night before, and we start our day off constructively.

Throughout the day we must check our thoughts by analyzing our emotions. We must properly evaluate our thoughts. We care for "self" by constantly asking, "What can I do to care for 'self?' " We become our own best friend, lover, and parent. We continuously discard our trash of negativity. When we feel down we lift ourselves up through meditation and positive visualization. As a result, we become empowered! We know how to tap into our source of joy anytime we are in need.

We take the necessary time to work on our weaknesses and improve our areas of strength. As a result, we become a better "self." We constantly look for ways we can become more efficient and more effective in accomplishing our goals.

We keep our eyes on the prize. We no longer allow people, places, and things to distract us. We surround ourselves with positive people, and we stay active, participating in healthy missions and causes.

We fill our minds with uplifting thoughts by purposely reading inspirational materials and monitoring the content of the material we take in. As a result, we feel good about ourselves and we stand in expectation to experience the good that is yet to come.

Chapter Questions

1) What activities can you do in the morning to ensure your day will start off right?

_____

_____

_____

_____

2) What activities can you do on your way to work, or on your way to your destination, to give you energy to get through the day?

_____

_____

_____

_____

3) What can you do to combat negative feelings when they approach?

_____

_____

_____

_____

4) What can you do to turn your situation around, if you encounter an obstacle during the day?

_____

_____

_____

_____

5) What can you do to sustain your peace, if someone tries to irritate you?

_____

_____

_____

_____

6) What areas do you need to improve on, that you have discovered on this journey?

_____

_____

_____

_____

7) What are your areas of strength?

_____

_____

_____

_____

8) What will you do to fix your character flaws?

_____

_____

_____

_____

9) How can you utilize your areas of strength to become a better person?

_____

_____

_____

_____

10) What have you learned about yourself from reading this book? Was this journey a beneficial experience for you? Why or why not?

_____

_____

_____

_____

Example

Ashanti woke up rattled by a nightmare she had the night before. She quickly regained her confidence as she awakened, and gave God thanks for seeing another day.

A big day lay ahead for Ashanti; she was going to take her GED test, which she had failed twice previously. Ashanti pictured herself successfully passing her test and became overjoyed by the concept of her achievement in her mind. As Ashanti began experiencing her joy, she rid herself of all the feelings of fear she previously had.

Ashanti became inspired as she dressed for school. She looked at herself in the mirror and said, "Ashanti, I love you." She smiled at herself. Ashanti got a cup of coffee and sat down to read her Daily Bread (daily devotional) and her Bible.

Ashanti then got into her car to go to school. There was an accident on the highway, so she ran into traffic. Ashanti didn't complain. She refused to let anything or anyone steal her joy. Instead, Ashanti turned on her CD player and listened to her favorite CD as she visualized passing her GED exam and being accepted into nursing school.

She imagined driving her dream car and living in her dream house. She saw herself working happily at her nursing job and having a good time with her family. She purposely savored each feeling of joy that came with the experience. Before she knew it, the traffic had cleared, and she arrived at school.

Ashanti went in, sat down, and took her test confidently. When a question seemed difficult, she took a deep breath and told herself, "Ashanti, you can do this!" She then became confident and answered the question.

The test was over and Ashanti felt a sense of accomplishment. She was sure that she had finally passed the test.

Ashanti left the test area and went into the lobby where she saw her friend Anna. Anna said, "Girl, we probably ain't never gonna pass this test. We don't need no GED, anyway."

"No, friend, this is it for me. I know I passed my test. I need my GED; I'm going to be a nurse. You wait and see," Ashanti said confidently to Anna as she detached herself from her.

Ashanti remained positive. She kept her eyes on the prize! As a result, Ashanti passed her GED with flying colors. She went to nursing school and today she is a successful LPN still looking to advance. Ashanti is no different than you and I. She made it a practice to keep focused on her success!

1) How did Ashanti combat her negative feelings from the nightmare she had?

_____

_____

_____

_____

2) What did Ashanti do to make herself feel good?

_____

_____

_____

_____

3) What did Ashanti do when she was confronted with traffic delays?

_____

_____

_____

_____

4) What did Ashanti do when she saw problems on her GED test that were difficult?

_____

_____

_____

_____

5) How did Ashanti handle her negative friend Anna?

_____

_____

_____

_____

Writing Assignment- Journal Entry #12

Write out a schedule of your day and the things you will do each day to work on "self." Include some of the techniques we discussed in this chapter.

DAILY SCHEDULE

Each Morning I Will:

Each Afternoon I Will:

Each Evening I Will:

If I follow this schedule, I will become a better "self!!!"

Journal

_____

_____

_____

_____

_____

_____

_____

_____

_____

_____

_____

_____

_____

_____

_____

_____

_____

_____

_____

_____

_____

_____

_____

_____

_____

_____

_____

_____

_____

_____

_____

_____

_____

_____

_____

_____

_____

_____

_____

_____

_____

_____

_____

_____

_____

_____

_____

_____

_____

_____

_____

_____

_____

_____

_____

_____

_____

_____

_____

_____

_____

_____

_____

_____

_____

_____

_____

_____

_____

_____

_____

_____

_____

_____

_____

_____

_____

_____

_____

_____

_____

_____

_____

_____

_____

_____

_____

_____

_____

_____

_____

_____

_____

_____

_____

_____

_____

_____

_____

_____

_____

_____

_____

_____

_____

_____

_____

_____

_____

_____

_____

_____

_____

_____

_____

_____

_____

_____

_____

_____

_____

_____

_____

_____

_____

_____

_____

_____

_____

_____

_____

_____

_____

_____

_____

_____

_____

_____

_____

_____

_____

_____

_____

_____

_____

_____

_____

_____

_____

_____

_____

_____

_____

_____

_____

_____

_____

_____

_____

_____

_____

_____

_____

_____

_____

_____

_____

_____

_____

_____

_____

_____

_____

_____

_____

_____

_____

_____

_____

_____

_____

_____

_____

_____

_____

_____

_____

_____

_____

_____

_____

_____

_____

_____

_____

_____

_____

_____

_____

_____

_____

_____

_____

_____

_____

_____

_____

_____

_____

_____

_____

_____

_____

_____

_____

REFERENCES

INTRODUCTION

Casarjian, Robin. House of Healing. Boston: Lionheart Press, 1995

CHAPTER ONE

Beattie, Melody. Codependent No More. Center City, Minnesota: Hazelden, 1987.

Narcotics Anonymous. California: World Service Office Inc., Van Nuys, 1988.

Williamson, Marianne. A Return to Love. New York: Harper Collins Publishers, 1992.

CHAPTER TWO

Beattie, Melody. Codependent No More. Center City, Minnesota: Hazelden, 1987.

The New King James Version Bible. Nashville, Tennessee: Thomas Nelson Inc., 1982.

Meyer, Joyce. Managing Your Emotions. New York: Hachette Book Company USA, 1997.

Williamson, Marianne. A Return To Love. New York: Harper Collins Publishers, 1992.

CHAPTER THREE

Beattie, Melody. Codependent No More. Center City, Minnesota: Hazelden, 1987.

The New King James Version Bible. Nashville, Tennessee: Thomas Nelson Inc., 1982.

Meyer, Joyce. Battlefield of The Mind. New York: Hachette Book Company, 1995.

CHAPTER FOUR

Beattie, Melody. Codependent No More. Center City, Minnesota: Hazelden, 1987.

The New King James Version Bible. Nashville, Tennessee: Thomas Nelson Inc., 1982.

Meyer, Joyce. Managing Your Emotions. New York: Hachette Book Company USA, 1997.

Narcotics Anonymous. California: World Service Office Inc., Van Nuys, 1988.

CHAPTER FIVE

The New King James Version Bible, Nashville, Tennessee: Thomas Nelson Inc., 1982

CHAPTER SIX

Beattie, Melody. Codependent No More. Center City, Minnesota: Hazelden, 1987.

The New King James Version Bible. Nashville, Tennessee: Thomas Nelson Inc., 1982.

Casarjian, Robin. House of Healing. Boston: Lionheart Press, 1995.

Meyer, Joyce. Battlefield of the Mind. New York: Hachette Book Company USA, 1995.

Meyer, Joyce. Managing Your Emotions. New York: Hachette Book Company USA, 1997.

CHAPTER SEVEN

The New King James Version Bible, Nashville, Tennessee: Thomas Nelson Inc., 1982.

Casarjian, Robin. House of Healing. Boston: Lionheart Press, 1995.

Meyer, Joyce.. Battlefield of The Mind. New York: Hachette Book Company USA, 1997.

CHAPTER EIGHT

Allen, James. As A Man Thinketh. Raddord, VA: Wilder Publications, 2007.

Byrne, Rhonda. The Secret. New York: Atria Books, 2006.

The New King James Version Bible, Nashville, Tennessee: Thomas Nelson Inc., 1982.

Meyer, Joyce. Battlefield of The Mind. New York: Hachette Book Company USA, 1997.

CHAPTER NINE

Beattie, Melody. Codependent No More. Center City, Minnesota: Hazelden, 1987.

The New King James Version Bible, Nashville, Tennessee: Thomas Nelson Inc., 1982.

Meyer, Joyce. Battlefield of The Mind. New York: Hachette Book Company USA, 1995..

Meyer, Joyce. Managing Your Emotions, New York: Hachette Book Company USA, 1997

Peale, Norman Vincent. The Power of Positive Thinking. Prentice Hall, 1996.

CHAPTER TEN

Beattie, Melody. Codependent No More. Center City, Minnesota: Hazelden, 1987.

Byrne, Rhonda. The Secret. New York: Atria Books, 2006.

CHAPTER ELEVEN

Canfield, Jack, Hansen, Mark, and Hewitt, Les. The Power of Focus.. Deerfield Beach Florida: Peale, Health Communications Inc., 2000.

CHAPTER TWELVE

Beattie, Melody. Beyond Codependency. Center City, Minnesota: Hazelden. 1989.

The New King James Version Bible, Nashville, Tennessee: Thomas Nelson Inc., 1982.

Canfield, Jack, Hansen, Mark, and Hewitt, Les. The Power of Focus. Deerfield Beach Florida: Peale, Health Communications Inc., 2000.

Peale, Norman Vincent. The Power of Positive Thinking. Prentice Hall, 1996.

About the Author

Jamila T. Davis, born and raised in Jamaica Queens, New York, is a motivational speaker and the creator of the Voices of Consequences Enrichment Series for incarcerated women. Through her powerful delivery, Davis illustrates the real-life lessons and consequences that result from poor choices. She also provides the techniques and strategies that she personally has utilized to dethrone negative thinking patterns, achieve emotional healing, and restoration and growth.

Davis is no stranger to triumphs and defeats. By the age of 25, she utilized her business savvy and street smarts to rise to the top of her field, becoming a lead go-to-person in the Hip-Hop Music Industry and a self-made millionaire through real estate investments. Davis lived a care-free lavish lifestyle, surrounded by rap stars, professional sports figures and other well known celebrities.

All seemed well until the thorn of materialism clouded Davis' judgments and her business shortcuts backfired, causing her self-made empire to crumble. Davis was convicted of bank fraud, for her role in a multi-million dollar bank fraud scheme, and sentenced to 12 1/2 years in federal prison.

Davis' life was in a great shambles as she faced the obstacle of imprisonment. While living in a prison cell, stripped of all her worldly possessions, and abandoned by most of her peers, she was forced to deal with the root of her dilemmas- her own inner self.

Davis searched passionately for answers and strategies to heal and regain her self-confidence, and to discover her life's purpose. She utilized her formal training from Lincoln University, in Philadelphia, Pennsylvania, along with her real-life post-incarceration experiences and documented her discoveries. Revealing the tools, techniques and strategies she used to heal, Davis composed a series of books geared to empower women. Davis' goal is to utilize her life experiences to uplift, inspire and empower her audience to achieve spiritual and emotional wholeness and become their very best, despite their dilemmas and past obstacles.

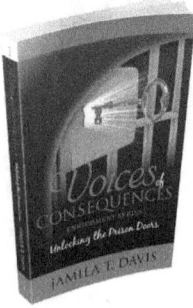

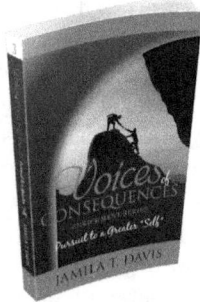

Voices International Publications Presents

$\mathcal{V}oices_{of}$
CONSEQUENCES
ENRICHMENT SERIES
CREATED BY: JAMILA T. DAVIS

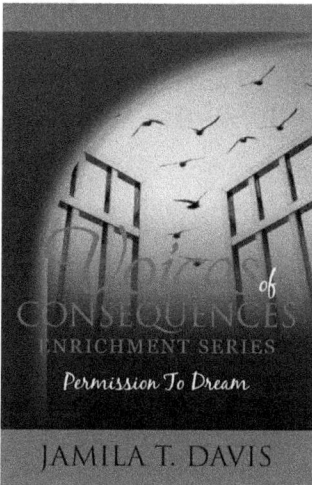

Permission to Dream: 12 Points to Discovering Your Life's Purpose and Recapturing Your Dreams

ISBN: 978-09855807-4-2 Textbook
ISBN: 978-09855807-5-9 Workbook/Journal
ISBN: 978-09855807-6-6 Curriculum Guide

Permission to Dream is a nondenominational, faith-based, instruction manual created to inspire incarcerated women to discover their purpose in life and recapture their dreams. In a way readers can identify with and understand, this book provides strategies they can use to overcome the stigma and barriers of being an ex-felon.

This book reveals universal laws and proven self-help techniques that successful people apply in their everyday lives. It helps readers identify and destroy bad habits and criminal thinking patterns, enabling them to erase the defilement of their past.

Step-by-step this book empowers readers to recognize their talents and special skill sets, propelling them to tap into the power of "self" and discover their true potential, and recapture their dreams.

After reading *Permission To Dream*, readers will be equipped with courage and tenacity to take hold of their dreams and become their very best!

VOICES
INTERNATIONAL PUBLICATIONS
"Changing Lives One Page At A Time."
www.vocseries.com

Voices International Publications Presents

$\mathcal{V}oices_{of}$
CONSEQUENCES
ENRICHMENT SERIES
CREATED BY: JAMILA T. DAVIS

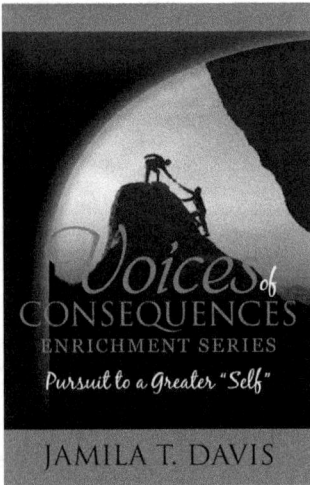

Pursuit to A Greater "Self:" 12 Points to Developing Good Character and HealthyRelationships

ISBN: 978-09855807-7-3 Textbook
ISBN: 978-09855807-8-0 Workbook/Journal
ISBN: 978-09855807-9-7 Curriculum Guide

Pursuit to A Greater "Self" is a non-denominational, faith-based, instruction manual created to help incarcerated women develop good character traits and cultivate healthy relationships.

This book is filled with real-life examples that illustrate how good character traits have helped many people live a more prosperous life, and how deficient character has caused others to fail. These striking examples, along with self-help strategies revealed in this book, are sure to inspire women to dethrone bad character traits and develop inner love, joy, peace, patience, kindness, generosity, faithfulness, gentleness and self-control. This book also instructs women how to utilize these positive character traits to cultivate healthy relationships.

After reading *Pursuit to A Greater "Self,"* readers will be inspired to let their light shine for the world to see that true reformation is attainable, even after imprisonment!

VOICES
INTERNATIONAL PUBLICATIONS
"Changing Lives One Page At A Time."
www.vocseries.com

VOICES
INTERNATIONAL PUBLICATIONS

ORDER FORM

Mail to: 196-03 Linden Blvd.
St. Albans, NY 11412
or visit us on the web @
www.vocseries.com

QTY	Title	Price
	Unlocking the Prison Doors	14.95
	Unlocking the Prison Doors Workbook/Journal	14.95
	Permission to Dream	14.95
	Permission to Dream Workbook/Journal	14.95
	Pursuit to A Greater "Self"	14.95
	Pursuit to A Greater "Self" Workbook/Journal	14.95
	Total For Books	
	20% Inmate Discount -	
	Shipping/Handling +	
	Total Cost	

* Shipping/Handling 1-3 books 4.95
4-9 books 8.95
* Incarcerated individuals receive a 20% discount on each book purchase.
* Forms of Accepted Payments: Certified Checks, Institutional Checks and Money Orders.
* Bulk rates are available upon requests for orders of 10 books or more.
* Curriculum Guides are available for group sessions.
* All mail-in orders take 5-7 business days to be delivered. For prison orders, please allow up to (3) three weeks for delivery.

SHIP TO:

Name: _____

Address: _____

_____

_____

City: _____

State: _____ Zip: _____